W9-BXU-937

FREDERICK COUNTY PUBLIC LIBRARIES

Unique Pets

SUGAR GLIDERS

Kristin Petrie

ABDO Publishing Company

visit us at
www.abdopublishing.com

Published by ABDO Publishing Company, PO Box 398166, Minneapolis, MN 55439.
Copyright © 2013 by Abdo Consulting Group, Inc. International copyrights reserved in all
countries. No part of this book may be reproduced in any form without written permission from the
publisher. The Checkerboard Library™ is a trademark and logo of ABDO Publishing Company.

Printed in the United States of America, North Mankato, Minnesota.
052012
092012

 PRINTED ON RECYCLED PAPER

Cover Photo: Photo Researchers
Interior Photos: Alamy p. 20; Corbis p. 17; Getty Images p. 11; Glow Images pp. 15, 21;
    Photo Researchers pp. 7, 9, 13, 19; Thinkstock p. 5

Series Coordinator: Megan M. Gunderson
Editors: Megan M. Gunderson, BreAnn Rumsch
Art Direction: Neil Klinepier

Library of Congress Cataloging-in-Publication Data

Petrie, Kristin, 1970-
  Sugar gliders / Kristin Petrie.
     p. cm. -- (Unique pets)
  Includes index.
  ISBN 978-1-61783-443-1
  1. Sugar glider--Juvenile literature. I. Title.
  SF459.S83P48 2013
  599.2--dc23
                              2012004890

Thinking about a Unique Pet?
Some communities have laws that regulate the ownership of unique pets. Be sure
to check with your local authorities before buying one of these special animals.

CONTENTS

SUGAR GLIDERS

What looks like a squirrel, soars through the air, and has a sweet tooth? This animal leaps like an acrobat, barks like a dog, and hisses like a snake. What could it be? It's a sugar glider!

The sugar glider is a marsupial. It belongs to the family Petauridae. The sugar glider's scientific name is *Petaurus breviceps*. Loosely translated, this means "short-headed tightrope walker."

The sugar glider has become a popular pet. Many fans are attracted by its small size and beautiful coat. And, its crazy gliding skills are quite entertaining! Keep reading to see if the sugar glider is the right pet for you.

Sugar gliders are related to koalas, kangaroos, and wombats. They all belong to the order Diprotodontia.

WHERE THEY LIVE

Sugar gliders are native to Australia, Papua New Guinea, and Indonesia. They are also found on Tasmania. Sugar gliders did not arrive in the United States until 1994.

Wild sugar gliders live in forests. They especially like eucalyptus forests. These trees produce sweet sap that gliders love to eat. Gliders spend their time gliding from tree to tree in search of a sugary meal. This is how sugar gliders got their name!

Yet life is not all gliding around and snacking on sap. Sugar gliders also need to rest. In the wild, they build leafy nests in tree hollows. Each nest is shared by a clan of up to seven adults and their babies.

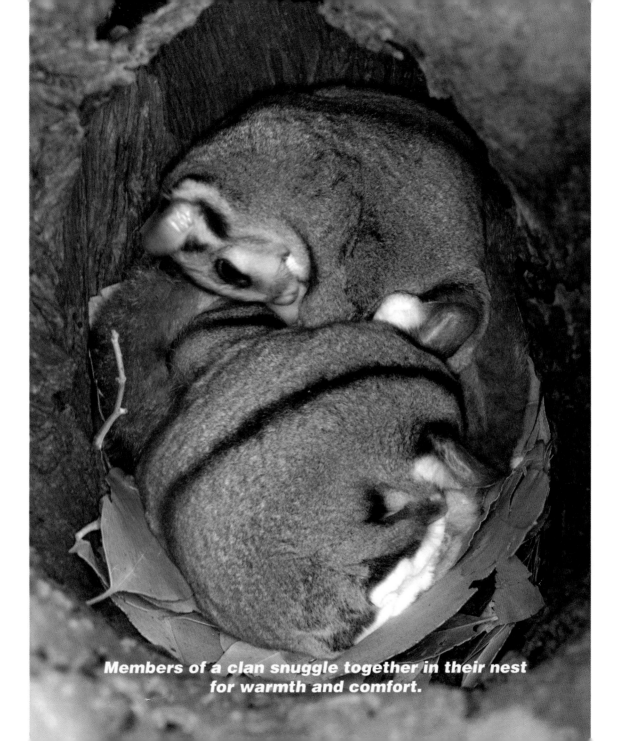

Members of a clan snuggle together in their nest for warmth and comfort.

DEFENSE

To secure the nest, dominant male gliders put their **unique** scent on each clan member. They also mark their territory. This tells sugar gliders from other clans they are not welcome there! Strangers are met with violent attacks and biting.

In the wild, sugar gliders also must watch out for natural predators. These include owls, cats, and **goannas**. Sugar gliders defend themselves by making loud noises, baring their teeth, and striking. They also stay off the ground. Even so, wild sugar gliders usually live just four to six years.

Unfortunately, gliding and **aggressive** behavior are no match against human threats. People capture sugar gliders to sell as pets. They also cause deforestation, which destroys the sugar glider's **habitat** and food supply.

Luckily, sugar gliders are considered "least concern" by the IUCN. So, they are not yet in danger of extinction.

WHAT IS THE IUCN?

The goal of the International Union for Conservation of Nature (IUCN) is to preserve the planet's varied species. For this reason, it supports numerous conservation efforts. Scientists assess the extinction risk of plant and animal species worldwide for the IUCN's Red List of Threatened Species.

Male sugar gliders have a scent gland on the head that looks like a bald spot.

WHAT THEY LOOK LIKE

A sugar glider is a tiny animal! Together, the head and body are just five to six inches (13 to 15 cm) long. A long, furry tail doubles the animal's length. Males weigh four to six ounces (110 to 170 g), which is about as much as a baseball. Females weigh slightly less.

Large, round eyes dominate the sugar glider's small head. A pointed snout narrows to a tiny pink nose. Two fairly large, hairless ears sit atop the head. Short legs taper to feet with clawed toes.

A thick, soft coat of fur covers the sugar glider's body and tail. Much of the coat is gray, but the belly is a cream color. A distinct black stripe runs between

the animal's eyes and down its spine. More black markings circle its eyes and ears. The tip of the tail is also black.

The sugar glider's most amazing feature is its patagium. It attaches to the sugar glider's wrists and ankles. This furry, kitelike membrane allows the sugar glider to soar through the air for up to 148 feet (45 m)!

When folded up, the patagium looks like a wavy line along the side of a sugar glider's body.

BEHAVIORS

Sugar gliders have a wide range of behaviors. They use body language, sounds, and actions to communicate. Gliders will stand on their back feet with teeth exposed when angry. They will bark to keep track of each other. What if gliders are hopping and spinning? Then they're happy!

Happy sugar gliders are curious and playful. In the wild, they enjoy soaring from tree to tree. In captivity, pet sugar gliders seek your attention. They love and need to be handled for at least two hours each day.

All this activity takes place at night, because sugar gliders are **nocturnal**. Their strong senses help them survive life in the dark. For example, their large, bulging eyes are set far apart and open very wide. This creates a wide field of vision. And, their ears move independently to catch every sound.

The sugar glider's tail provides steering and balance.

FOOD

The sugar glider spends much of the night in search of food. In the wild, it sails from tree to tree in search of sugary sap. But don't be fooled! These innocent looking creatures are omnivorous.

Sugar gliders eat plants as well as small birds, mice, lizards, and insects. They can even leap and catch moths in flight! Their sharp claws help them grab and hold on to these fast foods. Tiny fingers grasp the meal tight. Crunch, crunch, crunch! Sharp teeth do the rest.

A pet sugar glider should eat fruits, vegetables, and **proteins**. Meats, eggs, and insects are good sources of protein. Feed your sugar glider at night, since that is its natural time to eat. And, be sure plenty of fresh water is always available.

Tiny sugar gliders only need small amounts of food. Most eat between one-fourth and one-third of a cup (59 and 78 mL) of fruits and vegetables each day. They eat about one tablespoon (15 mL) of **protein**.

Keep a close eye on your sugar glider! Weight gain or loss will tell you if you need to adjust your glider's diet.

Eating the right amount of the right combination of foods is important to your sugar glider's health.

REPRODUCTION

After mating, a female sugar glider is only **pregnant** for 15 to 17 days. That's a very short time! The babies, called joeys, are extremely tiny at birth. They still have a lot of growing to do.

Mothers usually have two joeys at a time. After birth, the joeys climb into their mother's pouch. There, they drink their mother's milk while they continue to grow. They remain in the pouch for about 70 days. By then, it's getting crowded!

Seven to ten days after leaving the pouch, the joeys open their eyes. They still depend on their mother for care and feeding. By four to five months, they are ready for independence.

At this time, pet sugar gliders may be adopted. By this age, the joeys can eat well on their own.

If they are adopted later, they may have trouble adjusting to a new **environment**. So, the best time to bring your sugar glider home is just after **weaning**.

Both father and mother sugar gliders are attentive.
They will carry joeys on their backs or stomachs.

CARE

Patience is the number one thing needed to properly care for a pet glider. Sugar gliders recognize people by their scent. Once your glider knows your smell, it will remember and trust you.

Sugar gliders are very social animals. They will become lonely without company, so having two pet gliders is ideal. Is one your limit? Then handling your pet daily is even more important.

If you can have two or more sugar gliders, that's great! However, have males **neutered** unless you want many joeys.

For this, you will need a veterinarian who has experience caring for unusual pets. These vets can be a challenge to find. Make sure you have located one in your area before you bring a sugar glider home.

THE PET TRADE

Taking a sugar glider from the wild to sell in the pet trade can upset the balance of its environment. And, transporting an animal long distances can be harmful to its health. So, most people recommend buying sugar gliders from a breeder.

If you buy locally, you'll be able to make sure your glider has been bred in a clean, safe home. Ask the seller about his experience and have him provide references. He should ask the same of you. That way, you know the seller cares about where his gliders are going to live.

Avoid waking your sugar glider during the day. Waking it can cause stress, which may lead to illness.

THINGS THEY NEED

The first thing a pet sugar glider needs is permission to live in your house! Not all states or cities allow this type of pet.

If a pet glider is legal where you live, keep it in a large cage. The cage should be tall enough to hold long branches. This gives your glider room to climb.

Your sugar glider will also need a nesting box. This provides darkness for daytime

Be sure the cage is in a quiet area since these nocturnal animals need rest during the day.

rest. Bedding is not necessary, but shredded paper does make a nice cushion.

Snoozing in a shirt pocket or a pouch is a favorite activity!

Sugar gliders groom themselves to stay clean. So, they do not require bathing. But a clean nest and cage are important for good health. You must also wash food and water dishes daily.

Enjoy owning a glider! These entertaining pets are cuddly and easy to keep. Just be sure you are ready to give your glider the attention it needs. A happy, well cared for sugar glider will be a member of the family for 14 to 15 years!

GLOSSARY

aggressive (uh-GREH-sihv) - displaying hostility.

environment - all the surroundings that affect the growth and well-being of a living thing.

goanna (goh-A-nuh) - a large Australian monitor lizard.

habitat - a place where a living thing is naturally found.

neuter (NOO-tuhr) - to remove a male animal's reproductive glands.

nocturnal - active at night.

pregnant - having one or more babies growing within the body.

protein - a substance which provides energy to the body and serves as a major class of foods for animals. Foods high in protein include cheese, eggs, fish, meat, and milk.

unique - being the only one of its kind.

wean - to accustom an animal to eating food other than its mother's milk.

WEB SITES

To learn more about sugar gliders, visit ABDO Publishing Company online. Web sites about sugar gliders are featured on our Book Links page. These links are routinely monitored and updated to provide the most current information available.

www.abdopublishing.com

INDEX

2 1982 03035 2151